Lerner SPORTS

SPORTS
VIPs

MEET
TRAVIS KELCE

DAVID STABLER

Lerner Publications ◆ Minneapolis

SPORTS THRILLS *MEET* RESEARCH SKILLS

Lerner SPORTS

Free Database Trial: **lernersports.com**

Lerner Publications Company
An imprint of Lerner Publishing Group, Inc.
241 First Avenue North
Minneapolis, MN 55401 USA

For reading levels and more information, look up this title at www.lernerbooks.com.

Main body text set in Aptifer Slab LT Pro. Typeface provided by Linotype AG.

Editor: Annie Zheng

Library of Congress Cataloging-in-Publication Data

Names: Stabler, David author.
Title: Meet Travis Kelce : Kansas City Chiefs superstar / David Stabler.
Description: Minneapolis, MN : Lerner Publications , [2024] | Series: Lerner sports. Sports VIPs | Includes
  bibliographical references and index. | Audience: Ages 7–11 | Audience: Grades 4–6 | Summary: "Kansas City
  Chiefs tight end Travis Kelce is one of the best in the NFL. In the 2022–2023 season, he helped lead his team to
  victory in the Super Bowl. Explore his life and career"— Provided by publisher.
Identifiers: LCCN 2023017466 (print) | LCCN 2023017467 (ebook) | ISBN 9798765610473 (library binding) |
  ISBN 9798765623657 (paperback) | ISBN 9798765618028 (epub)
Subjects: LCSH: Kelce, Travis, 1989-—Juvenile literature. | Football players—United States—Biography—Juvenile
  literature.
Classification: LCC GV939.K36 S73 2024 (print) | LCC GV939.K36 (ebook) | DDC 796.332092 [B]—dc23/eng/20230518

LC record available at https://lccn.loc.gov/2023017466
LC ebook record available at https://lccn.loc.gov/2023017467

Manufactured in the United States of America
1-1009637-51720-7/6/2023

TABLE OF CONTENTS

>>>>>>>>>>>>>>

CLUTCH
PERFORMER

It was the Kansas City Chiefs' fifth game of the 2022 National Football League (NFL) season. The Chiefs were playing against the Las Vegas Raiders. Midway through the second quarter, the Chiefs were down 17–0. Things looked bad.

That's when Kansas City tight end Travis Kelce stepped up. He caught a pass from Chiefs quarterback Patrick Mahomes in the end zone. Touchdown!

FAST FACTS

DATE OF BIRTH: October 5, 1989
POSITION: tight end
LEAGUE: NFL

PROFESSIONAL HIGHLIGHTS: won the Super Bowl in 2020 and 2023; selected first-team All-Pro four times; has been a Pro Bowl player eight times

PERSONAL HIGHLIGHTS: grew up in Westlake, Ohio; starred on the TV show *Catching Kelce* in 2016; hosted *Saturday Night Live* in 2023

Kelce lands in the end zone to score a touchdown against the Las Vegas Raiders.

Kelce caught another two touchdowns in the third quarter. This gave the Chiefs a 24–20 lead. But he wasn't done yet. His fourth touchdown came during the fourth quarter.

The Raiders tried to catch up. But they were no match for Kelce and the Kansas City Chiefs. That day, Kelce scored all four touchdowns for the Chiefs in an amazing 30–29 victory.

The best tight ends can catch passes in tight spaces. Against the Raiders, Kelce totaled only 25 yards on seven catches. But he made each of those catches count. He tied the Kansas City record for most touchdowns in a single game. Kelce also set a record for an NFL tight end by scoring four touchdowns with only 25 yards. With his record-setting performance, Kelce showed why he was one of the NFL's best tight ends.

Kelce celebrates his touchdown against the Raiders.

TWO TOUGH KIDS

Travis Kelce was born to Ed and Donna Kelce on October 5, 1989. The family lived in Westlake, Ohio. Travis had one older brother, Jason. Travis and Jason were close. But when they played sports, the two boys both wanted to win. They always tried to get the upper hand on each other.

One day when they were teenagers, the brothers took their competition into the family kitchen. Travis had just won a game of basketball, but Jason claimed his brother cheated. Before long, their argument turned into a fight. It only stopped once their dad tried to break them up and pretended to get hurt.

Jason (*left*) plays center for the Philadelphia Eagles.

After winning the AFC Championship against the Tennessee Titans, Travis Kelce poses for a picture with his mom.

"I think that's when both of them finally realized they were equals and that they couldn't do this anymore," Donna Kelce said. "That was the end of it. No one picked a fight with the other one after that. It was over." Travis and Jason still competed. But instead of arguing, they pushed each other to be better.

The brothers played football at Cleveland Heights High School. Travis played quarterback while Jason played running back and linebacker. Travis excelled as both a runner and a passer. In his senior season, he ran for 1,016 yards and scored 10 touchdowns. He also threw for 1,523 yards and 21 touchdowns.

Colleges across the United States gave Travis offers to play football for them. He received offers from Akron, Eastern Michigan, Miami, and more. After thinking about his options, Travis accepted a scholarship from the University of Cincinnati Bearcats. It was a chance to play in his home state of Ohio. It also meant he'd get to play alongside Jason, who was already on the Bearcats offensive line. The brothers even began to dream they might make it to the NFL one day.

SUPER SPORTS SCOOP

Travis Kelce wears the uniform number 87 for the Kansas City Chiefs. The number is in honor of Jason, who was born two years before Travis in 1987.

ROAD TO THE NFL

In 2008, Travis Kelce arrived at the University of Cincinnati expecting to play quarterback. But the Bearcats coaches had a different idea. They saw Kelce's best position as tight end. "He was a big athlete, and he was tall," one of the coaches said. "For us, there was no question about it."

But Kelce was not ready to take on a new position just yet. He had never blocked a defender or caught a pass in a game before. These were important skills for a tight end. To prepare for his new position, he sat out his freshman year while he learned how to play tight end.

Kelce plays his first game with the Cincinnati Bearcats against the Rutgers

Kelce scores a touchdown for the Cincinnati Bearcats against Miami University in 2011.

Kelce was a hard worker. He stayed late after team practices to work on catching and blocking. By the start of the 2009 season, he was ready to go. He played as the team's backup quarterback and tight end.

Kelce caught only one pass for three yards that year. But he steadily improved over the course of the season. Kelce missed the 2010 football season. He was suspended for using an illegal drug.

Kelce returned to the field for his second full season with the Bearcats in 2011. He caught 13 passes for 150 yards and scored two touchdowns. Kelce and his coaches had high hopes for his final season at Cincinnati.

"I knew heading into his senior year that he could accomplish great things," said Cincinnati head coach Butch Jones. "You saw the true Travis Kelce come out in terms of leadership, toughness, and effort. He set the standard of what we believed in our football program."

Kelce tries to break through two Temple University defenders during a game in 2012.

In 2012, his last season at Cincinnati, Kelce set career highs with 45 catches and eight touchdowns. He also earned first-team all-conference honors. At the end of the year, Kelce was named the College Football Performance Awards Tight End of the Year.

Based on his outstanding senior season, the Kansas City Chiefs selected Kelce in the third round of the 2013 NFL Draft. The Chiefs' new head coach was Andy Reid.

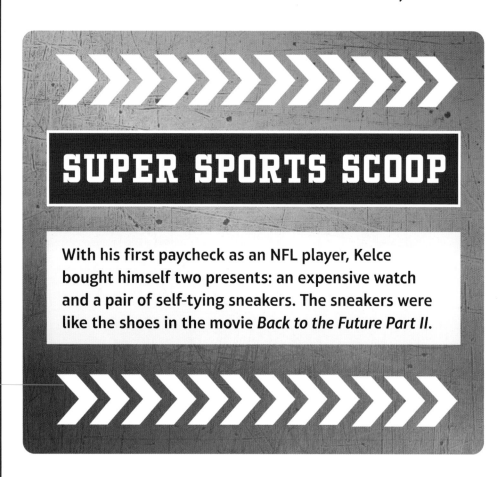

SUPER SPORTS SCOOP

With his first paycheck as an NFL player, Kelce bought himself two presents: an expensive watch and a pair of self-tying sneakers. The sneakers were like the shoes in the movie *Back to the Future Part II*.

Kelce (*top*) celebrates with teammates and head coach Andy Reid (*right*) during the 2020 Super Bowl.

Reid had drafted and coached Jason Kelce during his time with the Philadelphia Eagles. On June 6, 2013, Travis Kelce signed a four-year, $3.12 million contract. Reid looked forward to molding him into the NFL's next great tight end.

CHAPTER 3

CHASING A CHAMPIONSHIP

Kelce was looking forward to his first season in the NFL. But he would have to wait a little longer. Kelce injured his knee before the season started. After playing in just one game, he decided to have surgery to repair his knee. He missed the rest of the season.

Kelce worked hard to get better. By the fall of 2014, he was ready for his first full NFL season. He caught his first touchdown pass in the third game of the year and never looked back. For the rest of the season, Kelce was the Chiefs' leading receiver. He caught 67 passes for 862 yards. But the best was yet to come.

Kelce sprints down the field with the ball.

Kelce (*left*) high-fives Mahomes (*right*) after scoring a touchdown against the Denver Broncos.

In 2018, the Chiefs had a new starting quarterback, Patrick Mahomes. The hot prospect from Texas Tech University helped turn Kelce into an unstoppable machine. Kelce racked up 1,336 yards in 2018. He set an NFL tight end record for most receiving yards in a single season. He caught 10 touchdown passes and was named a first-team All-Pro player for the second time.

The Chiefs went into the playoffs with their sights set on the Super Bowl. They fell just short. But they had all the pieces in place for a championship run.

In the 2019 NFL season, everything came together for Kelce and the Chiefs. In an important playoff game, Kelce caught 10 passes for 134 yards. He also scored three touchdowns. The Chiefs came back from 24 points down to beat the Houston Texans 51–31. It was a comeback for the ages. "You just rally the troops, lean on the leaders of this team, and make plays," Kelce said. "That's what we did."

Kelce runs the ball into the end zone for a touchdown against the Houston Texans.

The win helped get the Chiefs into the Super Bowl for the first time in 50 years. The big game turned out to be no contest. Kelce caught six passes and scored one touchdown. The Chiefs won 31–20 against the San Francisco 49ers. The best tight end in pro football finally had a new title: NFL champion.

SUPER SPORTS SCOOP

Most teams have songs that play after they score. One of the Chiefs' victory songs is by the Beastie Boys. After winning the 2020 Super Bowl, Kelce gave an interview that mimicked the song's lyrics, "You gotta fight for your right to party."

CHAPTER 4

LET'S DO IT AGAIN!

With a string of record-setting seasons and a Super Bowl win, Kelce became one of the NFL's biggest superstars. He used his fame to do good and have fun.

Kelce gives one special fan the glove he used during a game.

Kelce started a program called Eighty-Seven & Running to help kids across the US. He also began Catching for a Cause to raise money every time he made a catch during the football season. This money would be used to help children through Eighty-Seven & Running.

In 2016, Kelce appeared in a TV show. He starred in the dating show *Catching Kelce* about his quest to find a girlfriend. Later, he and his brother also became cohosts of a sports podcast called *New Heights*.

On the field, Kelce had his sights set on a second NFL championship. Although the Chiefs returned to the Super Bowl for the 2020–2021 season, they were defeated by Tom Brady and the Tampa Bay Buccaneers. The Chiefs lost in the playoffs again the following year.

In 2022, Kelce set the pace for his teammates with a monster season. He made 110 catches for 1,338 yards and scored 12 touchdowns. He caught 14 passes in a win over the Jacksonville Jaguars to set a new NFL tight end record

Kelce scores a touchdown in the 2022 playoffs against the Jacksonville Jaguars.

for a playoff game. The Chiefs were going to another Super Bowl. But this time, the big game would be personal. Kansas City's opponents were the Philadelphia Eagles. Jason Kelce was Philadelphia's starting center. People called it the Kelce Bowl.

In the first-ever Super Bowl where brother faced brother, Travis Kelce came out on top. He caught six passes and scored a touchdown. The Chiefs won 38–35.

SUPER SPORTS SCOOP

After the Super Bowl, the Kelce brothers appeared together on the comedy show *Saturday Night Live*. In front of a TV audience of 4.5 million people, Travis and Jason got to clown around with the *Saturday Night Live* cast.

Left to right: Travis and Jason Kelce meet on the field after the 2023 Super Bowl.

After the game, the Kelce brothers shared a hug while their parents looked on proudly from the stands. Donna Kelce also came down to hug her sons. She had supported both by wearing a jacket that was half red for the Chiefs and half black for the Eagles. With two Super Bowl rings in hand, Travis Kelce proved once again why he was one of football's greatest superstars.

TRAVIS KELCE CAREER STATS

GAMES PLAYED:
144

CATCHES:
814

RECEIVING YARDS:
10,344

TOUCHDOWNS:
69

Stats are accurate through the 2022 NFL season.

GLOSSARY

draft: when teams take turns choosing new players

end zone: the area at each end of a football field where players score touchdowns

first team All-Pro: a team made up of the best players in the NFL each year

offensive line: the five players on offense who line up in front of the quarterback and block defenders

playoff: a series of games played to decide a champion

podcast: a program that people can listen to and download digitally

prospect: a player who is likely to succeed at a higher level of play

quarterback: the player who throws passes and runs the offense

scholarship: money that a school gives to students to pay for their education

tight end: an offensive player whose main job is to block players and catch passes

touchdown: a scoring play worth six points

SOURCE NOTES

10 Tom McManus, "Sibling Fights to Super Bowls: Kelce Boys Have Always Been Life of Party," *ESPN*, February 22, 2020, https://www.espn.co.uk/blog/philadelphia-eagles/post/_/id/29128/sibling-fights-to-super-bowls-kelce-boys-have-always-been-life-of-party.

12 Charlie Goldsmith, "Inside the 'Crazy' Story of How the UC Bearcats Turned Chiefs Star Travis Kelce into a Tight End," *Cincinnati Enquirer*, February 2, 2021, https://www.cincinnati.com/story/sports/college/university-of-cincinnati/2021/02/03/cincinnati-bearcats-turned-travis-kelce-into-tight-end/4309505001/.

15 Goldsmith.

21 Associated Press, "Chiefs Rally from 24–0 Hole to Beat Texans 51–31 in Playoffs," *ESPN*, January 12, 2020, https://www.espn.com/nfl/recap?gameId=401131043.

22 BarDown Staff, "Travis Kelce Alters His Beastie Boys Reference to Perfectly Suit Super Bowl Victory," BarDown, Accessed June 28, 2023, https://www.bardown.com/travis-kelce-alters-his-beastie-boys-reference-to-perfectly-suit-super-bowl-victory-1.1436947.

LEARN MORE

Anderson, Josh. *G.O.A.T. Football Tight Ends*. Minneapolis: Lerner Publications, 2024.

Anderson, Josh. *Inside the Kansas City Chiefs*. Minneapolis: Lerner Publications, 2024.

Kiddle: American Football Facts for Kids
https://kids.kiddle.co/American_football

Kiddle: National Football League Facts for Kids
https://kids.kiddle.co/National_Football_League

Sports Illustrated Kids: Football
https://www.sikids.com/football

Storm, Marysa. *Highlights of the Kansas City Chiefs*. Mankato, MN: Black Rabbit Books, 2020.

INDEX

PHOTO ACKNOWLEDGMENTS

Image credits: Cal Sport Media/Alamy, p. 4; Jason Hanna/Getty Images,
pp. 6, 7, 25; AP Photo/Perry Knotts, p. 8; Cooper Neill/Getty Images,
p. 9; Scott Winters/Icon Sportswire/Getty Images, p. 10; AP Photo/Chris
Bernacchi, p. 12; Jim McIsaac/Getty Images, p. 13; AP Photo/Al Behrman,
p. 14; AP Photo/Cal Sport Media, p. 15; AP Photo/Adam Hunger, p. 17; Joel
Auerbach/Getty Images, pp. 18, 19; Dustin Bradford/Getty Images, p. 20;
David Eulitt/Getty Images, p. 21; Maddie Meyer/Getty Images, p. 23; Jamie
Squire/Getty Images, p. 24; AP Photo/Kathryn Riley, p. 27.

Cover: Action Plus Sports Images/Alamy.